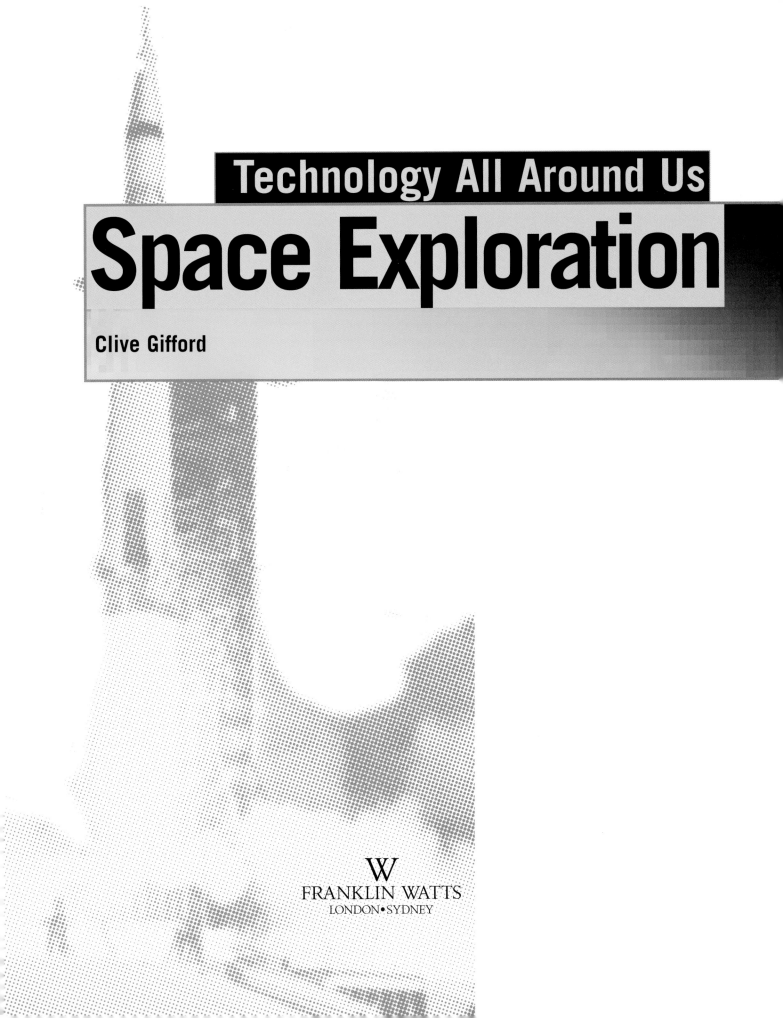

Technology All Around Us
Space Exploration

Clive Gifford

W
FRANKLIN WATTS
LONDON•SYDNEY

First published in 2005 by
Franklin Watts
96 Leonard Street
London EC2A 4XD

Franklin Watts Australia
Level 17/207 Kent Street
Sydney
NSW 2000

Produced by Arcturus Publishing Ltd,
26/27 Bickels Yard, 151–153 Bermondsey Street,
London SE1 3HA

Series concept: Alex Woolf
Editor: Alex Woolf
Designer: Tim Mayer
Picture researcher: Glass Onion Pictures

Picture Credits
Science Photo Library: 4 (NASA), 5 (NASA), 6 (NASA), 7
(NASA), 8 (NASA), 9 (Volker Steger), 10 (NASA), cover and 11
(Mike Agliolo), 12 (NASA), 13 (NASA), 14 (NASA), 15 (David A
Hardy, Futures: 50 Years in Space), 16 (NASA), 17 (Novosti),
18 (David Ducros), 19 (David A Hardy), 20 (NASA), 21 (NASA),
22 (European Space Agency), 23 (Johns Hopkins University
Applied Physics Laboratory), 24 (David Parker), 25 (David
Nunuk), 26 (NASA), 27 (Space Telescope Science Institute /
NASA), 28 (Detlev van Ravenswaay), 29 (Victor Habbick
Visions).

A CIP catalogue record for this book is available from the British
Library

ISBN 0 7496 5960 2

Printed in Singapore

Contents

Sending people or machines to explore space needs power, huge amounts of it. The power is needed to break free of the strong pulling force of Earth's gravity. Rockets are the machines for the job.

Technology in Action

Saturn V

It is 9 November 1967 and the world's largest and most powerful rocket ever launches successfully for the first time. The *Saturn V's* engines fire, producing more thrust than forty-eight Concorde supersonic airliners.

At over 110 metres in height, it is taller than a thirty-storey building and weighs three million kilograms. The Saturn V is made up of three stages. After the engines of each stage use up their fuel, they separate from the rocket and fall away.

Two years later, another Saturn rocket will launch the first Apollo mission to land a man on the Moon.

The launch of *Apollo 11* from Kennedy Space Center, Florida, on 16 July 1969 – the beginning of the first manned mission to land on the moon.

How Rockets Work

Rockets burn fuels stored inside their body and direct the huge amounts of thrust down at the ground. This thrust forces the rocket away from its launch pad and up through the Earth's atmosphere and into space.

Rockets have to work outside of the Earth's atmosphere where there is no oxygen to make a fuel burn. So they carry their own supply of oxygen, or a chemical containing oxygen called an oxidizer. Pumps mix the oxygen supply with the fuel before it is burned and the hot gases are forced out of the rocket's nozzles.

Increasing Power

A rocket's payload is the important object, such as a space station or a satellite, being carried into space. The first successful payload was the *Sputnik 1* satellite, launched by the USSR in 1957. It was a steel ball containing a radio transmitter and weighed 83.6 kilograms.

As rockets developed in power, larger and larger payloads could be carried. The *Saturn V* rocket could carry payloads as heavy as 118,000 kilograms.

American rocket pioneer Dr Robert H. Goddard, pictured in 1915. Eleven years later, Goddard built and launched the first rocket to be powered by liquid fuel.

Looking Back

Early Rockets

Small rockets using gunpowder were first developed by the Chinese over 750 years ago.

Space rockets were developed from rocket-powered missiles first used by German forces in World War II and then developed by the United States and the USSR. The first missions into space were launched by rockets that were converted missiles.

Rockets are single-use machines which launch their payload before burning up or becoming space junk. The space shuttle is the world's only reusable space vehicle. Built by NASA, the shuttle takes off like a rocket but lands like an aircraft on its return to Earth.

The first shuttle made its debut spaceflight in 1981. Since then, over 110 missions have been made by six different craft.

Safer and Cheaper

Shuttle missions have twice ended in disaster, in 1986 and 2003, with the death of all astronauts on board. Successors to the space shuttle are planned which aim to be safer and cheaper.

The *Challenger* space shuttle sits on top of a Boeing 747 jet. The shuttle is being transported from California to the Kennedy Space Center in Florida.

The shuttle takes between fifty-five and a hundred days to prepare for a mission. Future craft, such as orbital space planes launched from the top of a regular rocket, may take less than a month to prepare.

Take-Off and Touch-Down

As the space shuttle takes off, it is powered by two rocket boosters which are used up in just two minutes and discarded. For the next seven minutes, the shuttle draws fuel from a giant fuel tank, using 4,037 litres every second. Boosted high above Earth, the shuttle ejects the fuel tank and flies on into its orbit around Earth.

Working on the Shuttle

Circling the Earth once every ninety-two minutes, a space shuttle mission usually lasts seven or eight days. The crew of up to seven astronauts carry out experiments inside the craft and sometimes perform spacewalks outside.

The shuttle's cargo bay could hold a single-decker bus and is used to launch satellites, probes and other exploration hardware into space.

Hubble Trouble

It is 1993 and the fate of a billion-pound space telescope hangs in the balance. The Hubble Space Telescope (see pages 26–7) isn't working properly and a shuttle repair mission has been launched.

Millions watch on TV as, six hundred kilometres above Earth, the shuttle crew work round the clock. Over thirty-five hours of dangerous spacewalks outside the shuttle take place. But the mission is an outstanding success and the Hubble continues to work well to this day.

A view of the space shuttle *Atlantis*'s cargo bay. On this mission, the on-board observatory was to study the effect of solar radiation on the Earth's atmosphere.

In 1961, Russian cosmonaut Yuri Gagarin became the first human in space in a mission lasting just one hour and forty-eight minutes. Since that time, more than 450 people have entered space. Nearly all of these missions have been in craft orbiting the Earth.

Heavy Workload

Yuri Gagarin was little more than a passenger. He had next-to-no controls as he hurtled around the Earth.

On modern missions, astronauts have much more work to do. Instruments which study space have to be operated, experiments must be performed inside and outside the craft, and repairs sometimes need to be made.

Some spacecraft, such as the shuttle, carry equipment in their cargo bays which must be launched into space. On the shuttle, astronauts work with a robot arm that is over fifteen metres long. The arm can also help capture space hardware like satellites that are already in orbit, so that astronauts can repair or upgrade them.

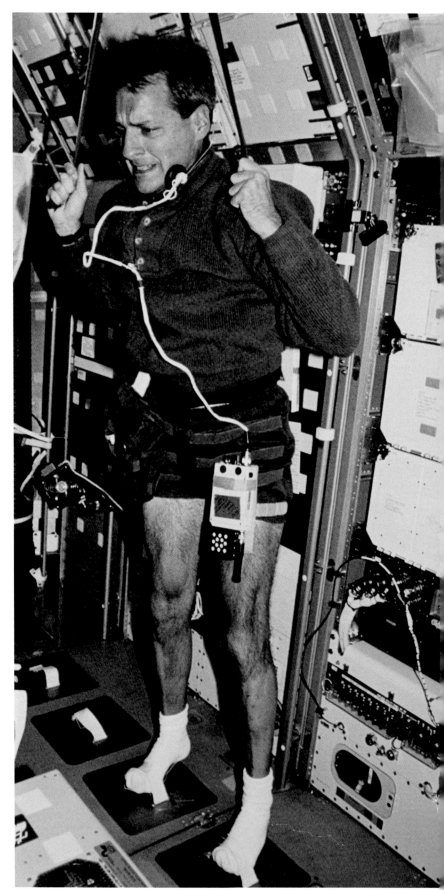

A NASA astronaut exercises on board the space shuttle *Columbia*. With his feet held in place by toe loops, he pulls down on straps to work his arm muscles.

Daily Chores

Crews in space experience microgravity, which makes them float around their spacecraft unless they are fixed in place. Restraints such as belts and Velcro fastenings keep objects and people in place. Daily cleaning prevents floating crumbs, dust and other debris from damaging the spacecraft's systems.

Weightlessness means that muscles don't work as hard as they do on Earth. Over long space missions, muscles can waste away unless crew members perform a regular exercise plan.

Right: This spinning platform is used to simulate the feeling of weightlessness astronauts feel when they orbit in space.

Looking Back

Space Snacks

The first food in space was healthy but not very tasty. It was made up of dried meat or vegetable cubes and liquid mush squeezed out of aluminium tubes. On the 1965 Gemini mission, American astronaut John Young smuggled a corn beef sandwich on board and received a telling-off as a result. Astronauts on the space shuttle get to choose from around a hundred different foods and drinks during their mission.

Looking Forward

Holidays In Space

In 2001, US businessman Dennis Tito became the first-ever space tourist. He paid twenty million US dollars for a trip on a Russian Soyuz vehicle which docked with the International Space Station.

Tito (along with several other companies) is working on plans to build a hotel in space, in orbit around Earth. Wealthy visitors would pay to fly by reusable space vehicle to the space hotel, which would offer spectacular views of Earth.

Spacewalk Systems

Inside their spacecraft, astronauts are safe and secure. Outside, in space, they need to be protected by advanced spacesuits when they perform Extra Vehicular Activity (EVA), known as spacewalks.

A Hostile Place

Space is a dangerous place for humans. There is no oxygen to breathe, but there is harmful radiation. Also, tiny dust particles called micro-meteoroids can rip through regular clothing and flesh.

Without the Earth's atmosphere to protect them, temperatures can soar to 122 degrees centigrade in the Sun's glare, and can drop to minus 180 degrees centigrade in the shadows.

The outer layers of EVA suits are tough to repel space dust, whilst inner layers are liquid-cooled and contain heating systems to keep an astronaut comfortable.

EMU Suit

Extravehicular Mobility Unit (EMU) suits are worn on space shuttle spacewalks. Made up of more than a dozen different layers, they take forty-five minutes to put on.

Looking Back

First Spacewalk

In 1965, Russian cosmonaut Alexei Leonov became the first person to perform a spacewalk. Disaster nearly struck when Leonov's spacesuit inflated and became too rigid for him to move. He had to release air pressure inside the suit and cram himself inside the inflatable airlock to survive.

Technology has improved greatly since Leonov's ten-minute spacewalk. In 2001, NASA astronauts Susan Helms and Jim Voss made a record spacewalk of eight hours, fifty-six minutes.

An astronaut being fitted into an EVA suit as part of his training. He will then be lowered into a deep pool of water to help simulate the weightless conditions of a real space mission.

EMU suits contain a main and emergency oxygen supply, which is controlled by a large backpack called the Primary Life Support System (PLSS). The PLSS also controls the temperature inside the suit and absorbs waste gases. Wearing an EMU suit, an astronaut can stay in space for seven or more hours.

Ready to Spacewalk

Suited up, astronauts go into a compartment called an airlock. Here they must wait for an hour or longer before they head out into space. This is to get their bodies used to the lower air pressure inside their suits.

Technology in Action

Untethered
It's 1984 and Bruce McCandless II becomes the first astronaut to make an EVA without a safety tether. He straps on the Manned Manoeuvring Unit (MMU), an advanced form of rocket pack which features twenty-four small thrusters.

For ninety incredible minutes, McCandless uses the joystick controllers on the arms of the MMU to travel through space, always keeping within a hundred metres of the shuttle.

Astronaut Bruce McCandless floats free above the Earth in his MMU.

Space Stations

Most manned spacecraft spend just a few days in space. Space stations, however, can spend months or even years orbiting Earth.

These large structures give astronauts the chance to perform lengthy experiments as well as letting scientists study the effects of living in space for long periods.

Russian cosmonaut Valeriy Polyakov stares out of the round window (centre) of the *Mir* space station. Polyakov's mission on board the space station in 1995–6 lasted 438 days.

Looking Back

Piece By Piece

The very first space stations – the twelve-metre-long *Salyut 1* (1971) and the twenty-five-metre-long *Skylab* (1973) – were built in one piece.

Since that time, space stations have grown in size and have to be transported into space in separate pieces. It is expected to take forty-five missions and around 1,700 hours of spacewalks to complete the 88.4-metre-long ISS.

Record-Breaking **Mir**

The first space station, *Salyut 1*, lasted less than a year in space and was lived in by a Russian cosmonaut for just twenty-three days. The *Mir* space station stayed in space for fifteen years and one crew member occupied the station for a record 438 days in a row.

A total of a hundred people lived and worked on *Mir* between 1986 and 1999. *Mir* was made up of six separate modules, including an observatory and a greenhouse. During *Mir's* lifetime, over 16,000 experiments were carried out on board the station.

Tricky Manoeuvre
It is 14 October 2000 and 360 kilometres above Earth a crucial piece of construction work is being carried out. A new docking port has to be put in place on the ISS – a tricky task.

A Japanese astronaut controls a robot arm to move the two-tonne port carefully past fragile solar panels with centimetres to spare. The delicate operation is a success. With the docking port in position, space shuttles can now park and connect with the space station.

The International Space Station (ISS) orbits some 360 kilometres above the Earth's surface. The giant solar panels (top) power all of its systems.

The International Space Station

The work of sixteen nations, the International Space Station (ISS) is the biggest structure put into space. When completed in 2006, it will weigh 450 tonnes and include six scientific laboratories.

It will be powered by its 108-metre-wide sets of solar panels. Astronauts have been living and working on the station since 2000. Over fifty thousand objects, from food canisters to tools and spare parts, will be found on the ISS. Each object is tagged with a tiny solar-powered transmitter.

13

Astronaut John Young leaps up from the Moon's surface after the *Apollo 16* lunar module's safe landing in April 1972. Young and fellow astronaut Charles Duke spent more than twenty hours on the lunar surface.

The Moon is our nearest neighbour in space. On average, it lies 384,400 kilometres away. The 1960s saw a race between the USSR and the United States to be the first to put a person on the moon.

The Eagle Has Landed

On 20 July 1969, Neil Armstrong and Buzz Aldrin stepped out of their lunar module, named *Eagle,* and became the first men on the Moon. During their twenty-two hours there, they collected twenty-one kilograms of Moon samples, before blasting off.

Their lunar module re-docked with the command module, which had been orbiting the Moon. As the craft approached Earth, the top part of the module separated and entered the Earth's atmosphere. It splashed down safely in the Pacific Ocean.

Looking Back

Crash Landings

Many of the earliest moon missions were designed to crash into the Moon, taking and sending back photographs before they were destroyed. In 1964, the American probe *Ranger* 7 took 4,308 photos before hitting the Moon. The previous six probes had all failed.

Between 1959 and 1976, there were thirty-one American and forty-eight Russian unmanned missions to the Moon. Around half of these missions failed.

An artist's impression of the European Space Agency's *SMART-1* spacecraft approaching the Moon. Launched in 2003, the probe is designed to observe and measure features of the Moon whilst staying in orbit.

 **Looking Forward**

Return to the Moon

A permanent base on the Moon could test out equipment and techniques which might be used to send people to Mars. A moon base might lie mainly underground to provide some warmth and a regular temperature.

Minerals from the Moon's surface could be mined and processed to create oxygen and useful materials. Plants could be grown in heated, inflatable greenhouses.

Search For Water

Just twelve people, in six Apollo missions, have set foot on the Moon. The last was Captain Eugene Cernan in 1972. But other missions to the Moon have taken place since. During the 1990s, two NASA probes, *Clementine* and *Prospector,* orbited the Moon. The probes found evidence that water ice may be found in craters near the Moon's poles.

Near Disaster

The 1970 *Apollo 13* mission was more than halfway to the Moon when an explosion damaged the craft's oxygen tanks and destroyed many of the ship's systems. Amazingly, the crew and ground staff were able to bring the spacecraft safely home.

Space probes are unmanned machines which explore parts of space and send back information to Earth using radio signals. Many of these probes have been sent to other planets in our solar system.

Looking Back

Photos Of Mars

The first successful mission to Mars was carried out by the US probe *Mariner 4*. In 1965, it flew by Mars at a distance of 9,800 kilometres and took twenty-two pictures. These were stored on a cassette tape and transmitted slowly back to Earth.

1996 saw the launch of *Mars Global Surveyor*. This probe got to within four hundred kilometres of the planet's surface. In 2001, *Mars Global Surveyor* took its 100,000th image of the planet's surface.

An image of Mars taken by the *Mars Global Surveyor*. The white, wispy clouds above the surface are believed to be made up largely of water ice.

Better than Humans

The eight other planets in our solar system are millions of kilometres away from Earth. It can take many years for a machine to reach them and there are dangers on the way.

Unmanned space probes can be built and sent on one-way missions with no hope of return. They can also be built far smaller and cheaper without the living quarters and the huge air, food and water supplies needed by astronauts.

Missions to Venus

Probes can survive hostile conditions on other planets. On Venus, for example, the surface temperature averages 460 degrees centigrade. The Russian *Venera 4* probe was the first to reach Venus's atmosphere. It was crushed by the planet's atmospheric pressure, which is ninety times stronger than Earth's.

Eight tougher Venera probes were more successful and explored the atmosphere and surface of Venus. Landing in 1982, *Venera 13* and *Venera 14* both used a series of drills to probe into the crust of Venus.

>> Looking Forward

Return Trips
Almost all probes to the planets head out on one-way missions, never to return. Future probes, however, are being designed to travel back to Earth carrying crucial samples of gases, dust, soil and rocks from other planets and moons in space.

A Mars Sample Return mission may launch in 2014, whilst Russia is planning to send a probe to collect soil from Phobos, one of Mars' two moons, by 2007.

A model of the *Venera 9* space probe, which entered the atmosphere of Venus in October 1975. The probe's lander successfully touched down on the planet's surface and sent back images and measurements.

A handful of space probes have travelled to the furthest parts of the solar system. These probes have massively increased our knowledge of distant planets like Jupiter, Saturn, Uranus and Neptune.

Far, Far Away

The longest-distance traveller of all is *Voyager 1*. It is now around 13.5 billion kilometres away from Earth. Weighing over a tonne, the probe contains 65,000 working parts. It was launched in 1977, but energy from its nuclear-power generator will keep it working until around 2020.

Voyager 2

Voyager 2 is the only probe to have reached and investigated Neptune and Uranus. *Voyager 2* discovered rings around Uranus similar to those found around Saturn. Together, the two Voyager probes discovered twenty-one new moons orbiting the planets.

Artwork of the Cassini-Huygens probe approaching Titan, one of Saturn's moons. The probe will orbit Saturn for some four years, sending back data about the planet, its rings and its moons.

Storms And Volcanoes

It is Spring 1979 and *Voyager 1* is travelling close to the solar system's largest planet, Jupiter. It returns 17,477 images of Jupiter and lots of other data from its eleven scientific instruments.

Back on Earth, scientists are excited by the discoveries. They learn that the Great Red Spot on the planet's surface is a huge hurricane storm, twice the size of Earth. They also see that there are active volcanoes on Io, one of Jupiter's moons.

This image shows the gravity assist technique used by *Voyager 2*. The spacecraft flew around part of Jupiter to speed it up on its way towards Saturn.

Gravity Assist

To travel great distances whilst using less fuel, many long-distance probes use a technique called gravity assist. This is where the probe flies round a planet and uses the pull of the planet's gravity to increase the spacecraft's speed.

The first spacecraft to use gravity assist was *Pioneer 10*. It flew to Jupiter at a speed of 9.8 kilometres per second (35,280 km/h). After flying round part of Jupiter, the effect of the gravity assist more than doubled *Pioneer 10*'s speed to 22.4 kilometres per second (80,640 km/h).

Looking Forward

Probe to Pluto

Pluto, the furthest planet from Earth, is the only planet not to have been investigated by a space probe. That may change with the future launch of the *New Horizons* probe, which might occur as early as 2006. Taking more than nine years to reach its target, the probe would investigate both Pluto and its mysterious moon, Charon.

Moving around the surface of the Moon or other planets is a real technological challenge. Yet a handful of rovers sent to the Moon and Mars have been highly successful.

Astronaut Eugene Cernan on board the Lunar Roving Vehicle, during the last manned mission to the Moon, in December 1972.

Moon Buggy

Astronauts on the *Apollo 15, 16* and *17* missions rode around the Moon's surface in a four-wheel-drive buggy called a Lunar Roving Vehicle (LRV). Two electric batteries powered the LRV to a top speed of 18.6 kilometres per hour. It could carry two astronauts, tools and rock samples and was fitted with a camera and radio antenna.

The First Rover On Mars

NASA's *Pathfinder* probe landed on Mars in 1997 and opened its body like the petals of a flower. Out rolled *Sojourner*, a small, six-wheeled roving robot. *Sojourner* was just sixty-three centimetres long and weighed only 10.5 kilograms, but it was very tough.

It carried several cameras and a large range of instruments with which it examined rocks and soils on Mars.

Water on Mars?

It's 2004 on Mars and a pair of NASA rovers named *Spirit* and *Opportunity* are nearing the end of their ninety-day main mission. *Spirit* approaches a ten-centimetre-high rock, codenamed Mazatzal, and begins to investigate it.

The robot uses a number of tools, including a RAT (rock abrasion tool), which grinds away the outer surface so that tests can be made on the clean rock underneath. Results suggest that there may have been water in the rock during its formation.

The Mars Exploration Rover, which roamed the planet's surface in 2004. The rover's mast contains cameras which give views of the Martian surface.

Looking Back

Lunakhod

In 1970, the Russian Luna 17 mission landed on the Moon, lowered a ramp and out rolled a bathtub-shaped rover called *Lunakhod*. Weighing 756 kilograms, the rover took 321 Earth days to cover just 10.5 kilometres of the Moon. The rover was remote controlled from Earth by five human technicians.

In 2004, the *Spirit* and *Opportunity* rovers, which weighed less than a quarter of *Lunakhod*, travelled around Mars. These advanced robots made many of their own navigation decisions.

Future Rovers

Designs for more than a dozen future rovers are being tested on Earth. One unusual design is called the Tumbleweed Rover. It is a two-metre-wide beachball-shaped machine which would roll over rocks and other obstacles in its path.

Comet and Asteroid Explorers

There are other bodies in our solar system besides the Sun, the planets and the Moon. Some amazing pieces of space technology have enabled scientists to learn more about these bodies.

Comets

A comet is a sort of huge, dirty snowball with a small, rocky core, in orbit around the Sun. Scientists are fascinated by comets and a number of probes have been sent to observe them in close-up. In 2004, the *Stardust* probe flew to within 240 kilometres of Comet Wild 2, the closest any machine has got to a comet.

Halley's Fleet

The most famous comet is Halley's Comet, which orbits the Sun once every seventy-six years. In 1986, the comet was examined closely by two Russian Vega probes, two Japanese probes and the European Space Agency's *Giotto* probe. These machines became known as Halley's fleet.

The nucleus of Halley's Comet, photographed by the *Giotto* space probe in 1986. *Giotto* came to within six hundred kilometres of the comet's nucleus.

Riding the Comet

March 2004 saw the launch of an ambitious comet chaser and lander built by the European Space Agency. The *Rosetta* probe is heading for Comet 67P Churyumov-Gerasimenko, seven billion kilometres away, and will reach it in 2014.

Once in orbit around the comet, *Rosetta* will drop the *Philae* probe onto the comet's surface. The washing-machine-sized lander will dig in spikes and then ride piggyback as it sends back information.

Asteroids

Asteroids are chunks of rock mainly found in a belt three hundred million kilometres wide, between Mars and Jupiter. Scientists believe they may be the remains of a planet which broke up.

Launched in 2003, the Japanese *MUSES-C* probe aims to briefly land three times on an asteroid to collect samples. The probe is expected to return to Earth in 2007.

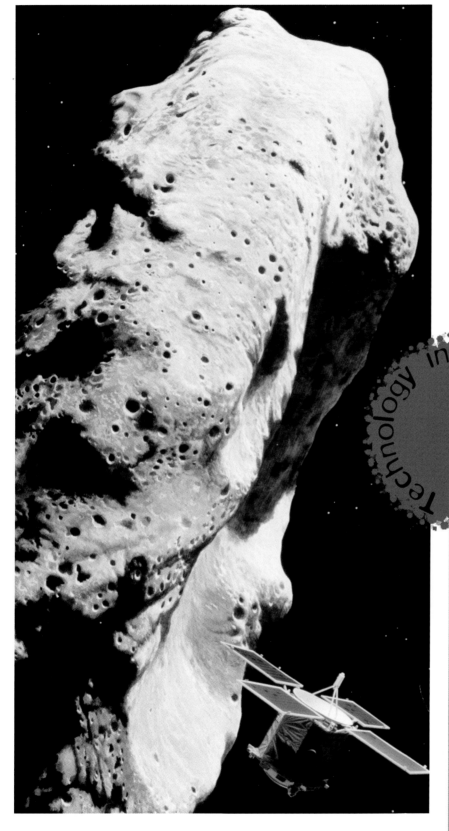

The *Near Earth Asteroid Rendezvous (NEAR)* space probe orbits Asteroid 433 Eros. The probe performed a ten-month survey of the asteroid, using a large range of cameras and scientific instruments.

Technology in Action

Asteroid Lander

It's 14 February 2001, and for almost a year the *NEAR Shoemaker* probe has been circling a large space rock called Asteroid 433 Eros. The probe has already taken over 150,000 photos. Now it is being asked to perform a mission it was not designed for.

The *NEAR* probe descends to the asteroid's surface taking sixty-nine close-up pictures. It then becomes the first machine to land on an asteroid. Amazingly, *NEAR* survives the landing to continue sending data back to Earth.

Telescopes have allowed people to peer into space and see things that are invisible to the naked eye.

Optical telescopes are used to collect and magnify light that can be seen by the human eye. Other types of telescope are used to collect radio waves, infrared and ultraviolet light and X-rays from space.

Refracting and Reflecting Telescopes

There are two types of optical telescopes. Refracting telescopes use glass lenses to magnify objects. Reflecting telescopes use large, smooth mirrors to collect light.

Telescopes are often measured by the size of the opening which receives light. The human eye has a seven-millimetre opening. Telescopes can have openings measuring one metre or more.

An astronomer uses a seventy-six-centimetre reflecting telescope at the Leuschner Observatory, near the American city of San Francisco.

Technology in Action

Collision Course

It is January 2001 and scientists are looking at signals collected by the Arecibo radio telescope in Puerto Rico.

The telescope spots and tracks an asteroid called 1950DA. This causes excitement as this asteroid was discovered fifty years ago but has been lost ever since. The scientists calculate that the asteroid will pass close by – or maybe crash into – Earth in the year 2880.

The VLT

Large telescopes are often placed in a building called an observatory with computers and other space instruments. The European Southern Observatory in Chile will soon house the Very Large Telescope (VLT). This is made up of four powerful telescopes all linked together. It will have the power to spot a small insect ten thousand kilometres away.

Radio Telescopes

Stars and other bodies in space give off radio waves. A radio telescope uses a large, bowl-shaped reflector dish to collect these waves. The signals are then often sent to computers to be processed and turned into images. Radio telescopes are often linked up to work together in what is called an array.

Looking Back

Planet Finder

In 1781, renowned British telescope-maker William Herschel was scanning the skies with one of his telescopes when he spotted an unusual object. For weeks he believed it was a comet before realizing it was a planet. Herschel had discovered Uranus. He had used a 17.8-centimetre reflecting telescope to make his discovery.

Astronomers today use much larger and more powerful telescopes. The Keck 1 reflecting telescope, situated in Hawaii, measures 9.8 metres.

A series of the dish antennae that make up the world's largest radio telescope, the Very Large Array (VLA), in New Mexico. The VLA consists of twenty-seven dishes, each twenty-five metres in diameter.

On Earth, telescopes have to peer through Earth's atmosphere. Out in space, clearer views and signals can be received. Telescopes have been sent into space, orbiting the Earth or travelling close to the Sun.

The Hubble Space Telescope is lifted out of the space shuttle's cargo bay by its robot arm after a servicing mission in 1997.

The Hubble Space Telescope

The most famous orbiting observatory of all is the Hubble Space Telescope. Work on the Hubble began fourteen years before it was launched into space in 1990. The Hubble features a 2.5-metre reflecting telescope, and instruments which collect and measure infrared and ultraviolet waves coming from distant stars and galaxies.

>> Looking Forward

The Hunt for New Planets

The search will soon be on for planets in other galaxies that might be capable of supporting life. NASA are planning to launch a new observatory, Terrestrial Planet Finder (TPF), between 2012 and 2015.

Featuring powerful telescopes offering a hundred times the detail of the Hubble, the observatory will seek out suitable planets and use instruments to measure their temperatures and identify the gases found in their atmospheres.

The Eagle Nebula
It is 1995 and six hundred kilometres above Earth the Hubble Space Telescope is capturing some of the most dramatic images of space ever seen. The telescope trains its instruments on a site seven thousand light years away – that is 450 million times the distance between the Earth and the Sun.

The Hubble photographs the Eagle Nebula – gigantic clouds of gas, billions of kilometres in size. Viewing the images on Earth, scientists are stunned by the sight of new stars being born in the Eagle Nebula.

An image from the Hubble Space Telescope of the spectacular Eagle Nebula. The "towers" of gas are over 900 million kilometres high.

The Hubble has sent back enough images and measurements to fill a personal computer every day for ten years. It has made 350,000 observations of stars and galaxies billions of kilometres away.

Observing the Sun

Launched in 1995, SOHO is an observatory which studies the Sun. Its instruments include a telescope which collects ultraviolet waves. Scientists use the data from SOHO to help them learn how the Sun and events in space affect the weather on our planet.

SOHO was meant to operate until 1998, but it was so successful that the European Space Agency and NASA decided to keep it running until 2007.

The Future In Space

Technology has so far only explored a tiny part of space. Yet the achievements in less than fifty years are impressive. The future is likely to see many more breakthroughs in technology and knowledge about space.

Living On Mars

Sending people to explore Mars may occur far later this century. It would be a huge operation involving many missions sending supplies, building materials and robots in advance of astronauts.

Joint Robotic Workforce

It is 2003 and in the United States important robots are being put through their paces. A pair of NASA robots which work together, called the Joint Robotic Workforce, practise moving steel girders and other building materials. A Frogbot practises leaping over large boulders. Small, mobile robots move in swarms, searching for objects and performing group tasks.

The successors to these test robots may all play a part in building a future Mars base before human visitors from Earth arrive.

A future base on Mars might be built out of parts shaped on Earth and transported to the planet in a series of space freighters, where they are put together with the aid of robots.

The astronauts would enter a set of buildings closed off from the hostile conditions on Mars. Such a place would need huge amounts of electricity supplied by nuclear power or giant arrays of solar panels.

Starships

To travel to the edge of our solar system takes many years. To travel to another solar system would take centuries unless new, faster ways of travelling through space can be found. Science will investigate lasers and other forms of energy in the future in order to build faster-travelling machines.

The Search for Intelligent Life

Is there intelligent life on other planets in the universe? No one knows, but the future will see more efforts made to search and make contact. The Search for Extraterrestrial Intelligence (SETI) looks for radio signals reaching Earth which may have been sent by alien life. One day, contact may even be made.

In the future, spaceships might be able to grow their own food and supply their own water and air. All waste would be recycled. Such spacecraft could travel huge distances for many years.

Looking Forward

Terraforming

Terraforming is the changing of a planet's environment so that it is sufficiently like Earth to allow people, plants and animals to live there. It is perhaps the most ambitious of all space projects and would take thousands of years. To terraform a planet such as Mars would need a large water supply. It would also need gases generated to form an Earth-like atmosphere which traps heat and warms the planet surface.

1957 The Soviet Union's *Sputnik 1* becomes the first satellite to be launched into space.

1958 The National Aeronautics and Space Administration (NASA) is founded.

1959 The Soviet Union's Luna satellite becomes the first to achieve an orbit around the Sun.

1961 Soviet cosmonaut Yuri Gagarin becomes the first person e...

1965 The first EV... Soviet co...

1966 Space p... (Luna... are t'...

1969 Apr... a...

1971 ... c...

1974 The Un... on the Apoll... American and Sov...

1976 *Viking 1* and *Viking 2* ... lander probes to send back ... surface of Mars.

1979 The *Voyager 1* and 2 probes reach Jupiter.

1981 The first space shuttle, *Columbia*, is successfully launched into space.

1984 The first untethered spacewalk is carried out by Bruce McCandless using a Manned Manoeuvring Unit (MMU).

1986 The space shuttle *Challenger* explodes, killing all seven astronauts on board.

1986 The first sections of the *Mir* space station are launched by the Soviet Union.

1990 The Hubble Space Telescope is launched.

1995 The European Space Agency's SOHO solar observatory is launched.

1996 A probe from the *Galileo* spacecraft examines Io, one of Jupiter's moons.

1998 Construction begins on the International Space Station, the largest human-made structure ever put into space.

2000 A crew begin living on board the International Space Station for the first time.

2001 The *Near Earth Asteroid Rendezvous (NEAR)* spacecraft becomes the first to land successfully on the surface of an asteroid when it lands on 433 Eros.

2003 The space shuttle *Columbia* explodes in flight, killing its seven-person crew.

2004 The Mars Exploration Rovers complete their mission on Mars.

asteroid A rocky object orbiting the Sun, mainly in a belt between Mars and Jupiter. The largest asteroid is around one thousand kilometres in diameter.

atmosphere The layers of gases that surround a planet or moon.

comet A small body in space made up of ice, snow and grains of rock and dust.

communicate Send and receive messages to people or machines.

cosmonaut An astronaut from the former Soviet Union or present-day Russia.

galaxy A collection of many stars, planets and gases bound together by gravity.

gravity The pulling force between objects.

hydraulics A power system using liquids in cylinders, found in some space machines.

light year A measure of distance in space. A light year is the distance that light travels in one year – 9,460,700,000,000 kilometres.

microgravity Very low gravity, as experienced by astronauts orbiting the Earth.

NASA The National Aeronautics and Space Administration. This is the organization in charge of all space programs for the United States.

orbit The path followed by an object in space as it goes around another object.

payload Important cargo which is carried on the space shuttle or a rocket.

planet A body in orbit around a star, such as our Sun.

radiation Energy that travels in waves.

satellite An object that orbits a planet or other body. Satellites can be natural, such as the Moon, or made by people, such as communications satellites which relay TV pictures around Earth.

solar system The solar system is made up of the Sun, the planets, their moons, asteroids and comets and any other dust or gas which is in orbit around the Sun.

star A massive, shining ball of very hot gas, such as the Sun.

terraforming The process of altering the environment of a planet or moon to allow it to support life from Earth.

ultraviolet ray An invisible form of energy which is given off by the Sun and other bodies in space.

Further Information

Further Reading

Eyewitness Guide: Space Exploration by Carole Stott (Dorling Kindersley, 2002)

The Facts On File Space and Astronomy Handbook by Joseph A. Angelo, Jr. (Facts on File, 2002)

Fast Forward: Space Shuttle by Mark Bergin (Hodder Wayland, 1999)

How To Live On Mars by Clive Gifford (Oxford University Press, 2001)

Moon Landing: The Race for the Moon by Carole Stott (Dorling Kindersley, 1999)

DVDs

Apollo 11: Men On The Moon (Twentieth Century Fox)

Mars: The Red Planet Collection (Brentwood Communications)

NASA: Fifty Years of Space Exploration (Madacy Entertainment Group)

The Planets (BBC Publishing)

Space (BBC Publishing)

Websites

http://kids.msfc.nasa.gov/Space/WhereTopics.asp
An up-to-date guide to where various rockets, satellites and space stations are currently in orbit.

http://www.seti.org/
The website of the Search for Extraterrestrial Intelligence Institute. This organization aims to learn more about life in space.

http://www.nasa.gov/audience/forstudents/5-8/features/index.html
A terrific collection of webpages from NASA aimed at students interested in space and space exploration.

http://www.historychannel.com/exhibits/moonshots/main.html
A detailed timeline of space exploration provided by the History Channel.

http://www.solarspace.co.uk/index.html
A website containing lots of information about the planets and features of the solar system and links to other space websites.

http://www.esa.int/esaCP/index.html
The homepage of the European Space Agency. Read about their past, present and future missions.

Index

Page numbers in **bold** refer to illustrations.